ABOUT TIME

ABOUT TIME
© Julie Benesh / Cathexis Northwest Press

No part of this book may be reproduced without written permission of the publisher or author, except in reviews and articles.

First Printing: 2022

Paperback ISBN: 978-1-952869-69-3

CoverDesign by C. M. Tollefson
Editing by C. M. Tollefson & Airea Johnson

Cathexis Northwest Press

cathexisnorthwestpress.com

ABOUT TIME

POEMS BY
JULIE BENESH

Cathexis Northwest Press

To Beau, patron of my arts, man-muse, cat-wrangler, and everything else

TABLE OF CONTENTS

STANDARD TIME	17
CARAPACE	18
THE COZY-KEEPER	19
3:00 A.M.	20
AFTER NEMEROV	21
CURRENT EVENTS	22
SPARE	23
CORPSE POSE	24
ON THE CONSTANCY OF FORGETTING	25
REMEMBERING THE SABBATH	26
AFTERLIFE	27
PROOF OF LOSS	29
WARMER	30
OVERTIME	31
GIRLWOR(L)D	32
SILVER-LINED APOCALYPSE	33
GOING COASTAL	34
WAVICLE	35
DIVORCE CASSEROLE	36
THREE DATES WITH HARRY CHAPIN: STORY SONGS	37
SHOW TUNES	38
KARMA, BY ANOTHER NAME	39
BEFORE WE MET	40
SINCE YOU'VE BEEN GONE	41
HOSPICE	42
IT'S OCTOBER	43
LOOKERS	44
THE INHERITANCE	45
MY MOTHER'S LAPIDARY	46
INJURED PARTIES	47
FACTS	48
CORNERSTONES	50
LAKE EFFECT	51
CHICAGO (AFTER GINSBERG)	52
I USED TO WRITE FICTION	53
THE POEM EVERYONE WRITES	54
HEAD TO TOE	55
FITTING IN	56

STANDARD TIME

Think of it as mood lighting. Even alpha Apollo
needs a rest. Even if you merry Christmas
with the best of them, strip a Christian and out pops
a naked pagan, pious in their own way, loins warming
by the fire. We are not equatorial, so follow

me as spring follows winter, slow yet relentless,
inevitable as death. The best holidays are clustered
where we need them, around the darkest times
of year when ritual promises renewal. *Cuffing
season*, the kids call it.

Fanning out to frame them, the glowing wreath
of minor constellations: Gothic Halloween,
shadowy Groundhog Day, and commercial cousin:
red-teddied, Valentine, shaking (martyred)
moneymaker; fractals equidistant between solstice
and equinox.

You say: summer bodies are forged in winter.
I say: we need energy to hibernate. Have more stuffing
and another piece of pie; let that blood drain brain to gut.
In six months time, that Great Lake —arctic,
berged with ice—will keep us cool,
while the rest of the city swelters.

CARAPACE

In the almost spring
as the white sky
tries to rain

Lana is afraid
of that empty Shell station
by the old highway exit,
like the cemetery at the end
of our block   its spirits,
yet fears no living exoskeleton,
ushering pests to safe new homes:
compassionate cockroach concierge,

whereas I murder by proxy with shrink-
wrapped, pre-shelled lobster meat
to throw on a charcoal grill
and consume in an act
of transubstantiation.

She does not yet know that Earth
is a graveyard.

It's all recycling, for better or worse:
the wages of life are shells;
the first currency, shells
hide, protect, outlast
their host. Fossils
make the world
go around; fossils,
fossils, the whole
way down.

That electric car billionaire plans
to abandon this space station:
Are we running out or moving on?

Lana believes in reincarnation; together
we ponder the immortal past: ghosts
of men in uniform, names squiggle-stitched
above their pockets, wiping windshields clean.

THE COZY-KEEPER

stains the burnished twilight fuchsia,
settling catlike on the warming lap
pressing fascia to bone, and bone to fascia,
brings gravitas to rest and rest to gravitas.

The cozy-keeper brews the warm elixir;
tea lights twinkle; unassuming
jewel tones spark festive feel, sans
frenetic force. Flows fragrant frankincense
as pulse and thoughts slow and strengthen,
brighten shadows, deepen depth.

The cozy-keeper rules the shifting shoulder
seasons: sweater weather, Halloween, Thanksgiving,
pumpkin spice! Presides on every rainy Sunday; that empty
space between the Solstice and New Year.
When moods are liminal, she is here.

The cozy-keeper spurs melodic memoirs: reveries,
dreams, reflections merge, diffuse—erasing
all temptation toward regret:
all now is to absorb, absolve, digest.
Her props: 1) tapestry 2) mirror, 3) mantle, 4) hearth,
5) lamplight, and 6) the cartoon clock whose whipping
hands now slow to stopping, until

O, miracle of cozy-keeping!

we, now timeless,
cease our fear
of dark and death.

After Thomas Lux's "The Joy-Bringer"

3:00 A.M.

Woke mid-poem: cool, clammy; dry mouth,
full bladder; burritoed in bedding,
thinking: constraint in art is called
form; holds substance together,
a working within. Whereas

growing up with an alcoholic
is a workaround: a dream
shanty incubating a future
that jumps genre. And

work is a body: ingesting, pulsing, pumping.
An open system evolving new-ish output every day:

marathon, menu, spreadsheet, symphony,
widget, gadget, jet... Yet, yes:

The universe is a vast bureaucracy
with hierarchies, networks, rules transparent
(as contronym). Whirring: *it is what it is,
it is what it is,* and muttering me back to sleep;
what happens is all that can.

AFTER NEMEROV

St. Howard would float down Lindell,
sink on Skinker, inches above the ground;
beaming dreamy, feeling groovy, like a mirror
blessing our youthful union. We called
him Uncle: it was all about us.

*Write what you know. That should leave
you with a lot of free time.*

We didn't know anything but the warm give
of our bodies; their sweet, swelling
scent. I tried to write poems
not knowing

A lot happens by accident in poetry

that journal they made fun
of, the one that took everyone
would not take me, so cursed
was I by joy.

I have a plot, but not much happens.

We didn't know
those years were but
a short break
from heartbreak.
Not the end.

*I sometimes talk about the making
of a poem within the poem:*

A bird's nest of dreams, detritus fused
with snot, tears; all that assorted effluvia.
It's not much, is it? But

*I love all my children even the squat,
ugly ones*

sacred enough for me now, the knowing, broken
Auntie beaming blessings of her own.

CURRENT EVENTS

Yesterday I scratched a mystery lesion
until I bled an iron scab on my arm,
my knee, my hand, my leg, my foot: no
comfort. Gunshots wake us at night, despite
our pricey property taxes: no rest.

That famous cupcake shop
has discontinued everything I like;
the restaurant has run out of sole
and waiters so we have to serve ourselves
filet mignon, and my belly won't fit
my underwear anymore, anyway: no digest.

I'm breaking   out beneath my wrinkles; hair
gentrifying from established to more dicey neighborhoods.
An insistent breeze may cause pelvic
congestion: no satisfaction.

Deja vu: a global adol-senescence
storming like *derechos*
before norming; peer pressure
sinking buildings: no stability.

People we thought we knew
and loved: canceled;
pasts exposed as lies
and sins, our consciousness
proven false: no traditions, no
nostalgia.

The techno-fix is a whack-a-mole
and we can't believe everything
we read, but what else is there?
They are selling big kid
pants, half off, at Nordstrom...
and the library?—still free:
no excuses.

SPARE

Spare me the organ recital
such music only decomposes
I want to know how not to be
ashamed of my panicula
my varicosities and lipid count
how not to trigger a spiral
        into worseness unto aboulia

Spare me your liturgy of forgetfulness
subtle arguments you draw
        that end in draws
your litany of filtered memories
like a junk drawer of dreams
you mistake for ours

Spare me your
semiotics of piety
to be a martyr is grave
    as victim is gravity
    as default

tell me how you talk yourself up
in the morning
down at night to sleep

under the same dark blanket
as the rest of us
the none of us who ever
were or ever will
be spared

CORPSE POSE

At the end of the day, on my way to yoga, the sun is yet to set, and no crepuscular rats dart through snowbanks like they did the night before, so far as I can see; the days are getting longer. First to the studio, I take my favorite spot, at the end, where I never used to want to be; hot yoga which I never used to think I'd like, but I love the routine of it unspooling as always: child's pose, sun salutations, lunges, warrior sequence, forward fold, tree, pyramid, goddess, locust, crunches, bridge, pigeon, happy baby, twists, legs up the wall. I sip my water and lie down for *savasana* imagining the sweet, spicy chai I will brew when I get home, and an essay I wrote this morning and I wonder whether the word "deficit" was I word I shouldn't have used, in that essay, and I am only supposed to think about "now," and my breath and my easeful body, not Past Essay and Future Chai, then it occurs to me, deficit can be another word for asset, just as surfeit can be too much extra, like a deficit of rats in the snowbanks is for me, better than a surfeit; and "now" can be longer, much longer, than the time it takes to walk two blocks through the snowy streets and brew a cup of chai, long as a late winter's evening, long as a life.

ON THE CONSTANCY OF FORGETTING

When I wake up and nothing hurts,
or something hurts in a soft way:
like a shin-twinge, radiating, muscular,
reminding me I can still break and come

back stronger, or even when a small
discomfort comforts: dry mouth, a rumble
of hunger or tingle of neuropathy, the civil
defense sirens silent, the sad trombones

and tiny violins mute as sleep, I remember
how I love when the weather forecast is wrong
in either direction, and how I thought physical therapy
was for the sedentary and then it cured my pain,

and while there may be no food in the fridge
there is food at the store my phone will pay
for with my job stress. I'm a good provider:
my silverfish are living their best lives,

feasting and weaving like wedding guests
in a painting by Breughel while the cats
pose decorative as Instagram royalty.
I have a panoply of invisible subscriptions

that no doubt keep the global economy
afloat. Also nothing's burning or even smells bad:
in my house or my fleshly abode: so much given
and chosen and dreamed and unimaginable,
the unlikelihood of any of us waking up

ever at all, let alone here and now together
in the careless flip of a blank new day
like no other and so many others: it's true
there are fates worse than clichés.

REMEMBERING THE SABBATH

When I get those Sunday scaries, those Sunday
scaries spreading dread like carbon monoxide,
low barometric pressure of the soul, and I want,

when I get those Sunday scaries, to avoid
a thousand dollars' worth of coral activewear,
consuming an entire French silk pie,

plucking bald brows, texting exes, hacking
hipster bangs, innovating new martini recipes,
to avoid Sunday scaries, I land on Google

Street View, seeking a glimmer, shimmer, trigger;
ghostly gasping greeting from the past places left
unattended: that strip mall I worked at during my divorce,

the condo where lightning struck like a bomb,
that gym where I worked off the frozen custard
from that shop with the peaked roof: imagining

current constituents suffering, suppressing Sunday
scaries: recreating, procreating, populating, tearing down,
clearing out, shoring up, like bellows reanimating, picking

up where I left off, until one scary Sunday in the future,
I will Google my current abandoned past present here,

in anticipation of anticipating
the anticipation of nostalgia,
remembering the Sabbath.
keeping it holy.

AFTERLIFE

I want to be everything you miss most:
your mother's red lipstick; the maid
with the soft hands and warm tongue,
your first love before she dropped her bag

and covered her eyes at the sight of your betrayal.
You say all our mistakes are behind us, born
again or aging out of misadventure, redeemed,
and it's true my dead cats come back new

and improved; and while the silver scar
on my collarbone is tender, my chopped meatball
heart beats slow and strong as a modernist's:
hardwired for progress.

I'm sure they ask it of all the agnostics:
if I'm so kind, how can I not be Christian?
But we are cannibals, not missionaries,
although if cannibals ever ate missionaries,

they surely became what they ate: missionaries
feasted on by cannibals feasting on themselves;
missionaries feasting on cannibals, projecting
savagery and sin.

The Buddhists remind us we lose/lose/lose, everything,
suddenly, or gradually and suddenly, and sometimes
it really is all your fault, but it might be the times you
least suspected: virtue signaled versus wisdom earned.

We are getting near the end, though maybe not,
and I want to die a morphine fiend like my M-browed
tabby, Mandy, my strategy shifting toward short-term rewards,
like a capitalist or hedonist, with characteristic lack of regret,

regret which, when excessive, in presence or lack,
becomes a parody of itself. We need to mourn
a bit for the future and the past to best love the here
and now, yet not so much we miss the point, the point

that having experienced heaven and hell
in this life, on earth, we should consider
that adequate preparation for whatever
happens next

PROOF OF LOSS

Princess Diana Was Alive For Hours...
the headline read... *just before she died.*
They had CCTV tapes: proof of life,
as if her passing hadn't come to pass.

We, that night, wedding guests at Tree of Life,
future scene of a hate crime two decades later:
eleven worshippers' loss of life.

That tabloid meant to say *Diana's Last Day
Caught on Tape*, still dramatic, but less haunting
than Schrödinger's Diana-cat, dead but alive
on the same godforsaken day, mere weeks

before our break up: me among the least
photographed women in the world,
in that snapshot wearing that black formal

that doesn't fit me anymore, my hand
on your arm, as if the very act of recording,
so contrary to its intention to preserve,
causes losses: foreshadowed, guaranteed,
of every possible dimension.

WARMER

All over my neighborhood, marching epaulets like bruises
branded as geese: turkeys, more like; flightless flocks;
uncoordinated armies of wannabe celebrities
justifying understated indulgence with a dramatic shiver.

A toasty torso is pointless when wind taps teeth like a mallet,
freezes hands, ice picks away at toes. My thrifty Chinese coat
with fleece and down and a dozen pockets
trapped my sweat so I gave it away. And that guy

with the Pomeranian wears just a sweatshirt
and Birkenstocks with wool socks; his dog
dressed warmer than him in boots and red sweater.

He's worried Pom will see a coat, goosedown-stuffed,
with coyote collar; sustainably sourced, trapped-not-farmed
and whimper:

Hey, that's my cousin.
Or: *I used to date her.*
Or: *Hey, there, on that guy's collar?*
That's my Canadian cousin
with whom I used to play-mate.
That sweet girl: oh, she was so wild!

OVERTIME

They no longer give kittens
away to the likes of me
and social media
generally approves.

It's one kind of pang to outlive
your animal companions,
but to think you won't
is next level.

Lord willing, those green bananas
will ripen in time, but they are only
.62 per pound.

All those trips I assumed were prefatory, preparatory
introductions? (Always leave something unseen to go back
to!-- like Delphi!) Most were last chances.
was it, is it, better to know or not?

Rare times I said to self: self, I will never,
ever do that ever again! Thank god!
Other times, abortive attempts,
realizing it's over, not even
remembering
the last time:

> Wear a bikini.
> Go on a first date.
> Work in an office.
> Job interview (?)

Pantyhose: the mass rebellion. My legs
itch remembering those plastic eggs
in the spinning rack at the drugstore,
early adopter of their cancellation.

May I never say: had I known I was going to live
this long I would have stolen that kitten.

GIRLWOR(L)D

Been every version of that girl:
first as an urchin I'd, furtive, twirl a curl
of hair and poke it in my ear: weird and impure.

Nerd, curmudgeon, hermit, lurking jerk, working
on curbing, purging her absurdest quirks,
but forth they burst, making it worse.

I've learned (and learned and learned)
it's best to spurn
attention, lest I hurl,
inspiring your so-called mercy-murders,
or incur some other, similar, familiar, curses.
So though I'm verbal, if not verbose, no verses
(plural) I've unfurled have gone viral
or curried any favorable furor
let alone commercial fervor,
and I remain and ever return,
alert, in that awkward spiral
of words heard and unheard.

So I endure your urgent burdens
as that hurdling, hurling, hurt-ling girl:
ardent, learned, undeterred
by those burnished purgatories
of your making   waiting, deter-
mined, unable to hurry victory, for the   turn,
the future fertile, febrile curdle I need to   earn
to occur, first,
before the   burn
and   urn.

SILVER-LINED APOCALYPSE

If you and I were the last people on earth,
I could, I would, make you love me.

I'd set all the standards and norms:
write my name in the sand on the beach
unless Instagram still worked, in which case
I'd do that.

I'd be an influencer, one of the top two;
share my fish with you; watch staggering insects
to find the best fermented berries.

I'd let you save me from whatever killed
everyone else, and if you needed some appendage
severed, I'd reluctantly assist. I'd tell you stories
and try to use all the words
we both had ever heard.

For various reasons, we would not propagate the species.
But we would adopt a bird, or something,
depending on what's available.

You might call it settling,
but I would call it nesting.

GOING COASTAL

Into the living room, through to the kitchen:

The house was brimming empty.

Soundless noise, intense absence. Outside, farm tools sat among

Sullen sparrows pecking under a willow by the red pump.

She was there alone:

Golden lashes framing wary eyes

Muscle twitching twixt ear and jaw;

Tang of pennies on the tongue.

She'd been waiting weeks for this

Encounter, but

None of that must show.

Out here, she was not

Powerless, only

Barren.

Here, she would watch water

Wending its way to the ocean.

Here, there would be a burial

At sea.

WAVICLE

Manometers measure pressure
but the act of observation
changes the observed. Bitter pattern
is like spewing iron dust on paper
over magnet, and a ghost traces remnants
of radiation that strayed.

Keepers preserve magnetism and latent
heat overcomes attractive forces.
Neutral equilibrium suggests stability but, *moi...*
I am not, by definition, a hot heat keeper, as vectors
measure distance, not displacement, i.e.,

we live together but are, indisputably,
alone and a wavicle is just a cute nickname for a photon:
wave plus particle, (sitting in a tree?) a tabloid's
celebrity couple's portmanteau.

Overtone is, likewise, strictly musical,
So perversion is not of unusual significance
and horizontal intensity is stable only in Britain,
fluctuating everywhere else, which makes no sense.

Cascade processes occur in stages (like cancer
in us animals, or irreconcilability in these makeshift
social pods we humans call marriage)

and damped ...oscillation...
slows ... itself ...down, whereas
entropy accelerates dis or der
grad u al ly,

Su d d e
n l
y.

DIVORCE CASSEROLE

Blanche when you get
served: you didn't see it coming; he's already
sampled every lawyer in town, leaving none for you.

Extract friends' knowledge of his
buffet grazing and
tasting menu. When did they
smell your marriage was ...put a
fork in it...
done?
(Beat it out of them, as needed.)

Spread rumors about his job or
mouthfeel:
serves him right!
Sift through your black and white memories.
Halve everything: all your
stuffing;
sweet and savory, breaking
bread with offspring and friends.
Reduce your
standard of living accordingly.

Scrape together
leftovers from fam and friends.
Salt with tears to
taste.

Fold.
Set aside: your differences for children and dignity.

Divide your grief into
ramekins where it won't
poison the whole
menu. Let it
cool until you can
taste it without
burning, until you can
measure all the ways each component
ingredient has sustained you:
raw, cooked, refined,
combined, separated.

THREE DATES WITH HARRY CHAPIN: STORY SONGS

December 14, 1977 Civic Center, Cedar Rapids Iowa: I Wanna Learn a Love Song
    I wore a chambray denim shirt with black velveteen collar and cuffs. L and I held hands in the cheap seats "*You can always count on the cheap seats!*" We were seniors in high school, in love, although we never said so, and he was into Harry.
    That spring L started playing soccer and quit calling me. Eventually he married one of our high school classmates, had two daughters, re-embraced religion and became a paperback writer.

June 28, 1979 Southern Illinois University Edwardsville Outdoors: A Better Place to Be
    It was my idea. I wore denim cut-offs and a gauzy white top. Hot and humid, and eventually a thunderstorm raged over. My college boyfriend B waited with me in line in the downpour for Harry to kiss me.
    Ended badly, when, a few months later I would meet the man I would marry.

April 24, 1980 Kiel Opera House St. Louis: Dreams Go By
    My 20th birthday. I made the plans and bought the tickets. I started crying mid-concert, because Harry was singing all the songs in the wrong order, and I felt responsible. I cried all over R's short sleeve button-down shirt, and he said he was honored. Just over a year later we eloped.
    A few months after that Harry died. I kept the mustard yellow T-shirt with the line drawing of a guitar for a long time.
    We got divorced, but I still feel like a widow.

SHOW TUNES

Ex texting
quotations, marked:
"*I know all about your*
standards..." Because July:
    Music Man.
last month was June's
    Carousel
bustin' out
all over.
(If I...)

Next month:
    State Fair
(Iowa, again, home state).

"*...Irish imagination...*" I know
he is drinking red
"*...Iowa stubbornness...*"
wine
"*...library full of*
books..." for his heart.

September, December
    Fantasticks.

May, always
    Camelot

Last line, un-
punctuated:
Don't you ever
think about being
...?

almost like being: it's always

Brigadoon   Groundhog Day.

KARMA, BY ANOTHER NAME

Babe?! Did you hear the clatter in the kitchen? The dog has gobbled down our dinner... again!

When we come back, from, you, know, *beyond,* one of us is gonna be him. We probably already were! We probably take turns as dog, me, you; you, me, dog; you, dog, me. Checks, balances; mutually assured preservation, life after life.

Comforting thought ...so... pizza or Chinese?

When in doubt, do both. Chianti, jasmine tea, potstickers...

...egg rolls, sausage and cheese, cannoli and fortune cookies.

Remember that place we used to go to finish each others'...
                ...meals?   Sentences!

Fornetto Mei. The pizza with the red grapes...We sat by the oven on cold winter nights, talking about Nietzsche, watching the cook with the little long-handled shovel?

Padddle...?

...*Peel*!

The husband was Italian, the wife Chinese; the food: not fusion, more ...

...eclectic.   ...complementary.

Well, but not free.

With an e...Remember in Paris? The bakery lady yelling "pas *compris*" when you snagged that macaroon...

Yin and yang? Like us?

...that sweet hot chili oil went with everything, made it all ...

...better, right!   ...*elevated.*

Like you!

Look who's complimentary...with an *I*!

BEFORE WE MET

From a decade away I could hear
the shimmer of heat from your barbecue.

I am sure you wish you knew me then.
I was that peckish princess: eyes

like plastic plates from Target;
dudes on the el   snapping/swapping/selling
pix of my sweet-sandaled feet.

That train
roiling me to sleep;
lulling me awake.

My hair, whiffing cilantro and ginger marinade,
would not quit growing under my crown,
convinced I would get what I wanted, so saucy
was I on the outside.

SINCE YOU'VE BEEN GONE

I rode that proverbial horse
to some more proverbial rodeos.
Back in the saddle.

I took those pills you wanted
me to. You got that operation.
Isn't it ironic? Which is not to say

coincidental, not at all. Quite the opposite.
Which is in itself ironic, so, same difference.
You thought I would starve or, at best,

find a sugar daddy to feed me ribeye
and frozen custard. But as I said at the time,
that's too easy. You know me: gotta do it my own way.

Since you've been gone I've mostly been begged
to stay— a few exceptions make the rule
credible; remind me of the standard

I set, the margin. Science is replicable; math
logical. That never changes. But humans
are of science without having to know science

much at all. I recall your hate for random weirdness
and your blindness to your own, the only kind
that really matters. You know what they say

about hindsight, how it twists every cliche,
like, well, you know what

HOSPICE

I want to die
a morphine fiend,
like my M-browed
tabby, Mandy. I made
a tent of striped fur, shot

her up; read her love
poems; sang lullabies.
She danced and chirped
her gratitude. No

Chemo—
(o, Mother!)
therapy.

Now I glimpse her
in every successive
cat, (as, I admit, my Major
Boyfriends sometimes blur
together in my synapses)

hoping you, love,
will likewise, not soon
but often, remember me.

IT'S OCTOBER

and, just back from the Farmer's Market, the last of the year,
I'm wearing a summer sweatshirt the amber and aubergine of falling leaves.
The cats mill expectantly, for what I know not. Behind the white and indigo clouds
the moon wanes. Because it's October, the saddle-colored boots I donned, first time since April,
have birthed a florid blood blister, like a plump strawberry, on my left inner foot,
so I wince-wobble, hydraulically suspended on a tender cushion of fluid shock
absorption I beg to break: in the shower, the soak, in my sleep.

It was October when I was eleven and my blisters got infected with yellow pus
and Dr. Reed lanced and drained them in his office, which my mother cleaned,
and he asked me, "Are you stupid?" Confused, thinking I was one of the smartest
kids in my grade, but if I really were stupid, mightn't I be wrong about that and not know?

My mother always asked me to examine her minor wounds, her cleaning lady bruises
and scrapes, and I would hurt her further by wrinkling my nose and saying "gross!" lacking
even my current level of ability to feign more empathic emotions. Stupid. One October a tumor
burst forth from her skin and as we read the mind of her home health nurse my mother
replied, don't worry, my daughter is so much smarter than I.

It's the October of my life, mathematically, actuarially; my mother died in her own October
and I have outlived her scarcely, so far. So, I pop my strawberry with a pin,
blotting away what looks like a nice vin rosé, leaving a hard callous.

It's October and at no time is it more obvious, even to the stupid,
that there are three seasons: past/present/future within each one,
but, how to bear a winter so barely begun?

LOOKERS

"Your ma has eyes in the back of her head." She'd laugh and laugh as I looked and looked.

Before he was my father, he ate carrots to pass the eye test to go to war. He met my mother-to-be on a double date with her foul-mouthed cousin with whom she lived. Later he'd wait for her to get home from dates with other boys, sitting on her porch and chatting with her aunt and uncle. She was an orphan, skinny then, but with those killer breasts (which would eventually kill her). He was a catch, the son of a judge, track champ, movie star handsome.

I hovered behind them; nascent, watching, rooting; desperate to inherit his looks, her insight; desire strong enough to get me born: a random mixed breed, compromised, derivative, half-blind.

She saw me: then, later, always, dragging my fingers across the back of her scalp, under her hair, imagining I could almost see them, wondering how I could possibly keep overlooking anything so important.

THE INHERITANCE

My dad fancied himself a philosopher, but his philosophy
was mostly Gleaned from message T-shirts,
The kind sold in kiosks instead of stores,
Humbly undeserving of a door or more than one wall,
max; just a counter, or, nowadays, a website.

He was a walking, talking meme before there were such things.
Intoning with mock grandeur, in italics, a pithy aphorism for every occasion:
Never a horse that couldn't be rode/Never a rider who couldn't be throwed.
Jesus: back by popular demand
I don't have a drinking problem: I drink, I fall down, I go to sleep—no problem!
His actual T-shirts, the ones he wore, were white, Fruit of the Loom;
What my mother would call his Holy Shirts, when they became more hole than shirt.
Eventually he would just wind them around his head and wear them as a bandana.
(*Waste not, want not!*)

What with the other quirks, it was hard to know if the drinking
was all that bad. "I never drink in *bars* like some people,"
he'd say. "That's because you're cheap," Mom would
reply. But today he'd be called a minimalist,
or an essentialist. He'd be on trend.

Maybe he was a philosopher after all, just born ahead of his time.
Maybe today, he'd tweet··· or write as short, as I do,
A form emphasizing the wholesome, holy hole,
I got from him.

MY MOTHER'S LAPIDARY

My mother didn't sew or knit or crochet
or embroider. She made rings
and belt buckles out of agates we found in the sand
That she never called gemstones, just rocks.

She tie-dyed Easter eggs and strung Christmas lights
That kept me awake forever.

She made my dinner, to order: Broiled lemon chicken,
Cubed steak sandwiches, baked potatoes
with sharp cheddar sauce, sour cream, and scallions,
before going to her night job as janitress.

Dad would fry bologna, later, sighing on the phone
to telemarketers, relatives, the occasional friend:
"I am making my own supper."
After eating he would turn to me and say:
"And now dessert, right?" Then he'd dunk
bread in maple syrup he made from boiled sap each spring.

He collected arrowheads, fossils, and coins
and taught me to hunt and gather morels,
which I called morsels,
and tried to teach me self-defense,
but I only learned to bicker and hide.

An excess of nothing but curation; I polish
and polish on the page and in my mind.

INJURED PARTIES

There is no [one]... however wise, who has not at some period... said things, or lived a life, the memory of which is so unpleasant... that [we] would gladly expunge it. And yet [we] ought not entirely to regret it, because [we] cannot be certain that [one] has indeed become... wise... – so far as it is possible for any of us to be wise – unless [one] has passed through all the fatuous or unwholesome incarnations by which that ultimate stage must be preceded.
MARCEL PROUST, Within a Budding Grove

I. When I was seven I told my mother that I sometimes had bad thoughts. She looked scared, like she was going to cry. Three decades later my Jungian analyst asked me if the bad thoughts had been sexual. No, they were about punishing people I didn't like, meaning people who had wronged or harmed me in some way. I put them in a cartoonish "Tunnel of Punishment" where they spun around, screaming. My mother asked no questions and the look on her face was my tunnel of punishment.

II. When I was ten I broke my wrist sliding down an icy hill at recess she told me not to. Actually, it re-broke because I thought of her and changed my mind halfway down and slammed my hand down to stop myself, and it obviously had not healed properly the first time, when I broke it roller-skating in my living room wearing a long nightgown. I told the school nurse that my mother would be sooo upset.

I did not mean angry. That had never occurred to me. But it turned out she *was* angry. Angry at what I said to the nurse, who had told her "not to be too hard" on me. This was not about frustration at being so misunderstood, or anger at being scolded, or any kind of embarrassment; she did not care much about purely social judgment. She thought I could be taken from her; that all my accident-proneness might look like child abuse. When I realized all this I woke her up in the middle of the night sobbing, and her stoniness was, again, not what I had expected.

When the plaster cast came off and I saw my pasty, scrawny arm, I wanted to vomit, or faint, but I didn't.

III. Teaching me to drive my dad yelled to brake and I hit the gas and the only tree for blocks in any direction. Without any more practice I nonetheless did OK in driver ed, because the dual controls made me feel confident. After I got my driver's license mom had me drive her around the block in the same old car with touchy brakes. I stopped too suddenly and the rickety rear-view mirror fell on her face and she was bleeding a little and I asked if I should pull over and she said no, she was fine, but she was shaking and crying while pretending not to, and I knew it was not about the minor cut, and it was definitely not about being proud and sad her baby was growing up – it was because she was afraid I never would, although, of course, I did.

FACTS

A cat's purr against your thigh builds dense bones
because to hum, sing, or skat is to convey all is well.
Like when I would wake up to my mother singing
and sweeping. When we would say good
night we would always add:
see you in the morning,

like throwing salt over our shoulders.
She taught me to fasten my boulder
holder the easy way, like they never
do in the movies: backwards, clasps
in front, pull it around, straps
up, no reaching around my back,
as well as to take it off from under my shirt
in the car or when I got home from work:
set 'em free, my husband would say.

Maybe some other mothers could command pets
vocally, but mine could send a menagerie
from every corner of the house, over to my side,
telepathically. Others might get wolf whistles,
but my gray-permed, double-knitted mother
had a neighbor kiss her full on the mouth
in front of my dad, myself, and a kitchen table
full of other startled onlookers. Other mothers
might serve snacks at Super Bowl parties, but mine?
She yelled, red-faced and hoarse as the men.

Teenage orphan, high school dropout, janitress, office
manager, bowling champion, fan of Jung, read Longfellow
to put me to sleep; taught me to read library books before kindergarten.
Killer cook. I used to tell her everything, a full-on, stream of consciousness
download when I got home from school, and while we tried
to take turns entertaining melancholy,
we more often ended up co-hostesses,
keeping one another company. But

recently we have had a hard time communicating; you might
say we have grown apart, lost touch, become estranged,
as it has been a few decades ago she died, and now
I'm older than her, so how to explain insurrection,
pandemic, terror attacks, or climate change,

let alone such complexities as my divorce,
to the serene, innocent deceased?

CORNERSTONES

Love and work are the cornerstones of our humanity – Sigmund Freud

Boys only want one thing, said Mom, with the killer breasts
that eventually killed her. (They couldn't help it; she didn't blame
them, the boys or the breasts.) Crushes will crush you; you will get pregnant,
drop out of school, be a single mother. (She dropped out but only to get married;
I didn't come along for years.)

I told Dad that when I grew up I'd have a job I liked and he said jobs
were what someone would pay me for, and what anyone liked was called a hobby.
Outlast the bad bosses and I'd be fine. He called me a Jill of all trades
and mistress of none; said if he messed up at work, airplanes
could fall from the sky; who could possibly *like* that?

She wanted me to be a boss, and mistress of myself. He wanted me to join the army
and study technology, not throw away my education on the ever-lovin' humanities.

A half century later they are both not *not* right:
it's an everyday miracle that anyone is born,
falls in love, or enjoys their career; that planes
stay in the sky or that breasts remain attached.

LAKE EFFECT

Lake Michigan is big and old as the universe. It keeps me hydrated and washed and flushed. It keeps me cool in the summer and warm (in my apartment) all winter, like board-shorted firemen whose bittersweet fragrance sings me to sleep. My sweetheart Beau says blah-blah *Ship and Sanitary Canal*, blah-blah *glaciers*, but I know what I don't know, and that ain't it; not a fan. The Lake loves me like Baby Jesus, Mother Mary and Bill Murray. Let science be science and God be God.

Forty-six years ago in a rented bus full of hormone-addled, sleep-deprived ninth graders I rode past my future, right by my current home, high (23 stories) on LSD (Lake Shore Drive) not even noticing its unprepossessing façade– like some kind of metaphor– blowing past my years-to-be in St. Louis, Naperville, Champaign, the marriage that took up my 20s, getting closer, closer to home.

Shelter is a roofless sky, an endless horizon where the sharp glow of clouds rain rainbows on the beach. At dusk I cross the Drive with my ninth grade self to catch fireflies on my tongue. Every cat and boy we've let rub up against us will follow, but that won't show up pictures, and we will never write any of this down. *C'est la vie*. The Lake will laugh, buoying up Bill Murray in board shorts forever and ever, amen.

CHICAGO (AFTER GINSBERG)

Chicago I fell in love with you at first sight in May 1975.
I wore that green dress and you wore the Lake.
You were the Big Man in the Midwest.
I was 15, you were 138.
Was it the age-gap Chicago?
I gave you the best years of my life when I thought you had given them to me.
All I wanted was to be an extra in any of your movies.
Are you gaslighting me?
I just wanted to grow old with you.
Even when my job went remote I stayed with you.
I don't know my sugar daddies from my F-boys I guess.
Chicago your machinery is too much for me.
How did I fail to notice?
I have been cheating on you with Cape Cod/Key West/ Santa Barbara/ Coronado/ Rome/ Berlin/ Dublin/ Paris and our bumpkin neighbor Door County.
How did you fail to notice?
Chicago do you even care so long as I pay my taxes?
These days everything in my brain turns into a blues poem. Urban country western.

Chicago I'm tired of defending you because it makes me sound codependent and pathetic hitching my wagon to a flashy con man.
Your rep is so bad you are gonna get canceled.
You just sold one of your newspapers to a hedge fund and I can read the graffiti on your wall.
Has Navy Pier swallowed you?
At least you still provide every citizen with their own pet rat and optional illegal firearm courtesy of Indiana.
Chicago I worry you are my soulmate and I don't know it or that I think you are but you aren't.

Chicago I did not sign up to be your sugar mama your nurse with a purse now did I or maybe I forgot I keep forgetting how forgetful I am getting.
Everyone on Next Door is already gone looking down from their perches in Schaumburg and Florida still obsessed with you.
My 99 Walk Index Score is no longer keeping me warm at night.
Chicago I always loved your sense of humor but not everything is a joke.
What was the moment it all started to go wrong when Ritchie sold the parking or way back in Council Wars?
If we break up I'll take the theatres and you can have all the sports.
Chicago I know the edges beyond your sweet ganache lakefront were always hard and rough.
I'm not a fool just a fool for you.
Chicago I feel like it's gonna be me or you and I'm still not sure whose side I'm on.

I USED TO WRITE FICTION

I was never skinny enough to be a poet
and prosody gave me math anxiety.
It seemed like there were more
rules, and ways to be wrong,
in poetry.

Strangers liked my fiction
but my friends started gossiping
about my protagonists' proximities
and similarities and adjacencies: *well,*
they are all just like you, except you
don't; you never; you haven't; it's not,
but otherwise... (they **never** saw
themselves), and my exes said

well, that's not exactly how it went down:
(they **always** saw themselves). And I said... fiction!
But it was not the truth to which they objected,
it was the fib: Why not just call it fib-tion?
Plus short stories

are quite long and flash so flashy, so then I wrote micro-memoirs
which hardly anyone got. Plus, was I really there, for my own conception?
Fibtion, again. Now my friends and exes and strangers either say they love
poetry or that they don't get poetry, and now I can just stop,
catch myself, right
        in the mid
        dle of a li

THE POEM EVERYONE WRITES

is the one about passing time: those old movies
where wind blows the calendar pages and clocks
run down; the commercials where kids
grow up in an instant or morph
into their paunchy parents.

But there's that other poem that stops time
like a snapshot that is not your wedding
or anything designated special. Just a leaf, a tear,
a wave: a moment in its universal uniqueness,
which is also about passing time:

movies, clocks; kids morph parents; time;
wedding, tear, uniqueness;
time.

HEAD TO TOE

I'm not a girl; I'm a professor of students middle-aged who call me doc,
when I wish they didn't. Yet known for my hair and footwear,
then and now. Then, as expected: shiny surfaced
middle-parted brunette. Saddle shoes red v. black. Clogs.
Goth boots. Edged out peers Later: blonder, smarter,
more degreed. Wiser, grayer; hence, with assistance, blonder.
Smarter meant better jobs; more money:
better shoes and hair— virtuous cycle.
Now what's beneath the scalp and skull,
expected (more or) less so platform
snakeskin wedge-heeled booties on fleet feet
of forever nerd with fierce blonde mane
that at height of heels, peak of highlights
a colleague hate-flirted he wanted to wear, like a pelt, on his belt.
        Spun, shocked, sobered—thought he'd appreciated inner brilliance.
Knew then, I'd be sad when hair, footwear,
inevitably descend to finally full-on sensible, but goddess
must, above all, at every cost, preserve the feet
for firm and mobile foundation,
the mind for all else.

FITTING IN

Sorry I didn't regret that I did it! Leading sweet
with fuchsia penuche, crashing the slumber
party in my modest lingerie; semicolons askew,
dreaming D-listers spooning me to sleep,
massaging my shoulders to salsa.

Sorry not sorry I am not a fan of football;
I will never understand the droning roar;
the roaring drone. It must require beer—
is that it? In my next life I will be normal,
like Miami, sinking slow *mojitos bonitos*.

The following poems were published previously, some in slightly different forms, in these journals:

Another Chicago Magazine: "Since You've Been Gone"

Beyond Words: "Facts," "GirlWor(l)d," "I Used to Write Fiction," "The Inheritance"

Black Fox Literary Magazine: "Corpse Pose," "Head to Toe"

Cathexis Northwest Press: "3:00 AM," "After Nemerov," "Afterlife," "The Cozy-Keeper," "Divorce Casserole," "Going Coastal," "Proof of Loss," "Silver-Lined Apocalypse," "Spare," "Warmer," "Wavicle," (as "Wave")

Cleaver: "Show Tunes"

Closed Eye Open: "My Mother's Lapidary"

Dillydoun Review: "Injured Parties," "Karma by Another Name," "Overtime," "The Poem Everyone Writes," "Remembering the Sabbath"

Griffel: "Before We Met"

Havik: "Lake Effect"

HASH: "Lookers"

House Journal: "Current Events" (as "News")

JMWW: "Standard Time"

New World Writing "Three Dates with Harry Chapin"

Prometheus Dreaming: "Cornerstones," "Hospice"

The Scapegoat Review: "The Constancy of Forgetting"

Sky Island Journal: "Carapace"

The Write Launch: "Chicago (After Ginsberg)," "Fitting In," "It's October"

Julie Benesh is a midwesterner by geography and temperament. She grew up in Iowa and has lived in Chicago for many years. She has published stories, poems, and essays in Tin House, Crab Orchard Review, Florida Review, Another Chicago Magazine, Hobart, JMWW, Cleaver, Maudlin House, Sky Island Journal, and many other places. She is a graduate of the MFA Program for Writers at Warren Wilson College and the recipient of an Illinois Arts Council Grant. Julie earned bachelor's degree in English from WashU in St. Louis, her M.S. in management and organizational behavior from Benedictine University, and her PhD and MA degrees in human and organizational systems from Fielding Graduate University. She enjoys concurrent careers as organizational consultant, professor of organizational leadership, higher education leader, creative writing instructor, and career and creativity coach, but she'd rather be reading or writing. Lately she's been doing a lot of conference presentations on the intersections between poetry and organizational psychology. Read more at juliebenesh.com.

Also Available from Cathexis Northwest Press:

Something To Cry About
by Robert Krantz

Suburban Hermeneutics
by Ian Cappelli

God's Love Is Very Busy
by David Seung

that one time we were almost people
by Christian Czaniecki

Fever Dream/Take Heart
by Valyntina Grenier

The Book of Night & Waking
by Clif Mason

Dead Birds of New Zealand
by Christian Czaniecki

The Weathering of Igneous Rockforms in High-Altitude Riparian Environments
by John Belk

If A Fish
by George Burns

How to Draw a Blank
by Collin Van Son

En Route
by Jesse Wolfe

sky bright psalms
by Temple Cone

Moonbird
by Henry G. Stanton

southern athiest. oh, honey
by d. e. fulford

Bruises, Birthmarks & Other Calamities
by Nadine Klassen

Wanted: Comedy, Addicts
by AR Dugan

They Curve Like Snakes
by David Alexander McFarland

the catalog of daily fears
by Beth Dufford

Shops Close Too Early
by Josh Feit

<u>Vanity Unfair and Other Poems</u>
by Robert Eugene Rubino

<u>Destructive Heresies</u>
by Milo E. Gorgevska

<u>Bodies of Separation</u>
by Chim Sher Ting

<u>The Night with James Dean and Other Prose Poems</u>
by Allison A. deFreese

Cathexis Northwest Press

www.ingramcontent.com/pod-product-compliance
Lightning Source LLC
Chambersburg PA
CBHW030138100526
44592CB00011B/936